Goalkeeping

Contents

England's Ben Foster about to launch an attack.

INTRODUCTION

Brilliant Brazilian goalkeeper Marcos turns the ball round the post.

WANTED: A COOL HEAD

Goalkeeper is one of the most important positions on the pitch. He or she is the last line of defence – and often the first line of attack. To be a good goalkeeper you will need courage, a cool head, quick reflexes – and a loud voice! You will need to 'boss' your own defenders, perhaps to tell them when an opposing forward has been left unmarked.

If you think you can handle it, you're halfway there. Confidence is important. So too is a clear understanding of the job, the rules of the game and the skills you need to be a better player.

You are unique and important. You might not be able to win a game by scoring a goal, but you could still be the match-winning hero by keeping out the other team. You might even make a winning save in a penalty shoot-out.

This book teaches you the basics – how and when to catch or punch the ball, where to position yourself, and how to become the best goalkeeper you can be.

Diagrams and pictures take you through a series of drills to sharpen your skills with one or more friends – and you will have a lot of fun doing them.

Remember, it takes a lot of hard work and practice to get to the top in anything – and goalkeeping is no exception!

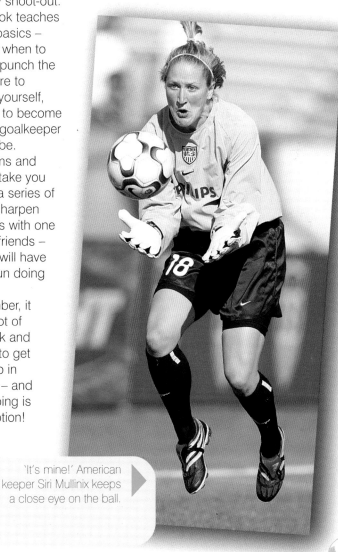

'It's mine!' American keeper Siri Mullinix keeps a close eye on the ball.

PROFILE OF A **GOALKEEPER**

Goalkeepers are like well-built cars – they go on for ever. While most outfield players hang up their boots at age 35, top goalkeepers can still be at their peak at 40. Often the difference between a good keeper and an outstanding one is experience. The younger you start, the more you can learn, so get that No. 1 jersey on now…

Sometimes groups of youngsters playing a game in their local park will pick teams, only to find no-one volunteers to go in goal. Someone gets thrown the gloves – or the job is shared among teammates, with each taking a turn between the posts.

Every player should try being a goalkeeper to see if they have a passion or a natural talent for it.

WHAT MAKES A GOOD GOALKEEPER?

- Calmness under pressure
- Confidence
- Courage
- Quick reactions
- Being decisive
- Being mobile and athletic

Gianluigi Buffon, of Italy, saves a shoot-out penalty – every goalkeeper's dream!

DID YOU KNOW?

Walter Zenga, of Italy, went 517 minutes (almost six games) without letting in a goal in the 1990 World Cup finals, beating the record held by England's Peter Shilton.

It can be lonely when the action is at the other end of the field, but good goalkeepers are always involved. They watch the play move round the pitch, they are quick to spot any danger – and they make sure they are in the right position to save. Good keepers make the job look easy.

Of course it takes a lot of practice, even if you have natural talent. But you can make all the difference to the result of a match.

After a few successes, you will be keen to be your team's No. 1 every week – even if someone else decided you should be in goal in the first place…

THE **STANCE**

Success comes from learning the basics. That's why we start with the stance. Get it right and many of the other skills will fall into place.

This keeper is in the correct stance. Here are the key points to remember:

- Stand on TIP-TOES

- FEET shoulder-width apart

- HANDS at waist height

- BALANCED BODY – your weight should be even on each foot

- KNEES forward, slightly bent

- EYES on the ball.

PRACTICE NO.1

This exercise needs two players. Mark out a goal and pitch, as shown in the diagram on page 7. Cones are ideal, but sticks, bags, drinks bottles, or even jackets will do!

Your friend, the attacker, has the ball and dribbles it slowly from left to right, starting at the first corner marker.

As he moves across the face of the goal, he turns to face the goal every few seconds and threatens to shoot.

The goalkeeper's task is to 'shadow' him by moving across, opposite the attacker. Each time he threatens to shoot, get into the 'good stance'.

You should get a feel for the 'good stance' and be ready whenever you expect a shot.

Ready and waiting: The goalkeeper takes up the ideal stance.

Practising your stance.

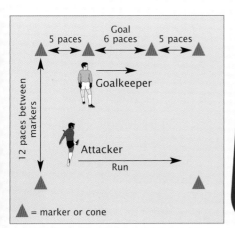

5 paces | Goal 6 paces | 5 paces

12 paces between markers

Goalkeeper

Attacker

Run

▲ = marker or cone

BE THE BEST

- The goalkeeper should not jump sideways. He should 'slide' across – almost like a crab – always keeping in contact with the ground so that he can react instantly.
- When the Attacker threatens to shoot, 'freeze' in the ready stance.
- Have five goes, then swap positions.

HANDLING THE **BALL**

There are three important rules a goalkeeper should always follow when handling the ball:

1. Get your body behind the ball whenever possible.
2. Gather the ball to your chest to protect it.
3. Cushion the ball gently – you do not want it falling away from you.

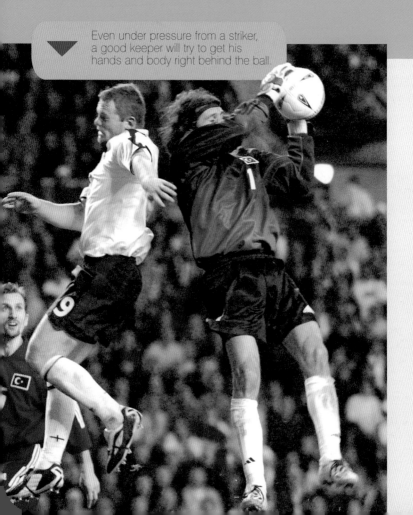

Even under pressure from a striker, a good keeper will try to get his hands and body right behind the ball.

Kneeling technique:
Keep your hands and
legs behind the ball.

GROUND SHOTS

There are two ways to collect the ball from the ground – either stoop forward or kneel down behind the ball. The position of your head, hands and feet are very important. When you stoop, keep your feet together so the ball doesn't slip between your legs.

	Stoop technique	**Kneeling technique**
Feet	Close together	Sideways kneel
Hands	Behind the ball, palms out, then cup the ball to chest	Behind the ball, palms out, cup the ball to chest
Head	Steady, eyes follow the ball	Steady, eyes follow the ball

WAIST-HIGH SHOTS

Only the position of the feet changes here. Good habits come as much from what you do with your feet as with your hands...

Feet	Shoulder width, weight equally balanced on either foot
Hands	Palms outwards, cup to waist/chest
Head	Steady, eyes follow the ball

CHEST-HIGH SHOTS

Not a lot of difference here from dealing with the ball at waist height. Relaxing the chest is important – as the ball can bounce away if you stand too rigidly.

Feet	Shoulder width, weight balanced
Hands	Palms outwards, cup ball, relax chest
Head	Steady, eyes follow the ball

BALL ABOVE THE HEAD

Even great goalkeepers have been left embarrassed by failing to gather a high ball cleanly.

Sometimes in a game, you will be under pressure from opposing attackers. You may even have your own defenders in your way.

Having a safe pair of hands when the ball is in the air will give your team confidence.

Feet	Shoulder width, weight equally balanced on either foot
Hands	Behind the ball forming a W-shape with the thumbs, relaxed fingers, secure ball into the body.
Head	Steady, eyes follow the ball

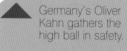

Germany's Oliver Kahn gathers the high ball in safety.

Spread your fingers behind the ball.

HANDLING PRACTICE

Measure two goals, three paces wide, ten paces apart. Two play, and you will both be goalkeepers.

- Throw the ball to each other in turn. The first five times, make sure the ball goes along the ground.

- The next five throws should be below head height – but above the ground.

- Have five more turns, this time tossing the ball above head height.

The next stage:

- Throw the ball to each other, just like the last exercise, again not kicking it.

- Have another 15 throws each, but this time, mix up the order to include five high, five low, and five at chest height, so the other player doesn't know what to expect. Remember the good stance and what you should do with your hands and feet.

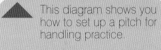

Goalkeeper 1

Goalkeeper 2

Goal
← 3 paces →

10 paces

▲ = marker or cone

This diagram shows you how to set up a pitch for handling practice.

GO FOR IT!

Keep the other player guessing where you will throw the ball.

DID YOU KNOW?

Spare a thought for Nicky Salapu of American Samoa. He let in 31 goals in a World Cup qualifying game against Australia.

NARROWING THE **ANGLE**

You can't make your goal smaller, but you can perform an amazing 'magic' trick to make your goal seem smaller to an attacker. If you stay on your goal-line when he approaches you with the ball, he'll have a big space either side of you to shoot at. But, if you come out towards him, you will 'narrow the angle'. It makes the gaps either side of you appear smaller, giving the attacker less of a target to hit. Coming off your line to narrow the angle also gives you more chance to stop any shot. The attacker will have to hit the ball closer to you to score.

Off your line:
Suddenly the
target has shrunk
for the attacker.

DID YOU KNOW?

Real Betis keeper Joaquin Valerio was once sent off 40 minutes before his team's Spanish Second Division game with Albacete. He insulted the referee in the tunnel...

PRACTICE NO. 1

You will need some strong string, rope, or elastic, about 25 paces long. Tie one end to one goalpost, and the remaining end to the other post (see the diagram below).

- The attacker stands 12 paces away, with the rope round his back, stretched tight.

- As the attacker moves from side to side, he will always be the same distance from goal. When he moves across, so does the keeper.

- The attacker then stops, or 'freezes' from time to time. So does the goalkeeper, who should be able to just about touch the rope with each hand outstretched while in the good stance position.

- Have ten 'freezes' each.

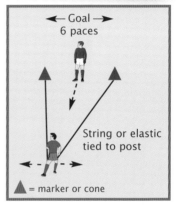

The attacker moves from side to side, and the keeper moves forward to narrow the angle.

BE THE BEST

When you both 'freeze', the attacker should allow the goalkeeper to correct his position so he can just touch the rope with either hand.

GO FOR IT!

Slide your feet as you move from side to side so that you are in contact with the ground at all times.

SHOT **STOPPING**

It is the last minute of an important match and your team is a goal ahead – but under heavy pressure from the other team. You pull off a superb, diving save. You are the hero – even though you did not actually score the winning goal. Moments like that can make all your hard work worthwhile. It is important that, when diving to your side, the hand nearest the ground should be directly behind the ball and your other hand should be slightly on the top of the ball, to prevent it from coming free.

 The fans behind the goal think it's in... but the keeper gets the ball to safety, over the bar.

Safety tip: Get your hands behind and slightly on top of the ball like this.

PRACTICE NO. 1

Set up a goal six paces wide. An attacker takes up a position about 15 paces away.

BE THE BEST

Try to get your body behind the ball. If you cannot, try to get your hands to it, behind and slightly above.

- The goalkeeper serves the attacker, who must control the ball, move it a couple of paces and shoot.

- Have 10 shots each – the most saves wins!

To make this drill even harder have another friend act as a defender. The defender stands five paces away from the goal post and passes the ball to the attacker. As soon as the ball is halfway to the attacker, the defender can join in and stop the attacker scoring. Have five attempts each.

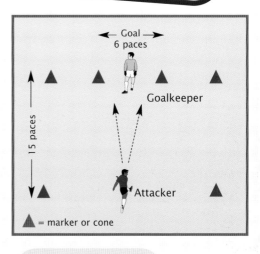

Goal → 6 paces

15 paces

Goalkeeper

Attacker

▲ = marker or cone

This diagram shows you the drill for shot stopping.

COMING OFF YOUR **LINE**

A goalkeeper often has to make quick decisions. There is no substitute for experience, but good coaching and practice will help you become a better goalkeeper. One of the biggest decisions you will have to make is whether you should come off your line. A pass is played between the last defenders and an attacker is clean through with just you to beat! You have to decide: 'do I stay where I am – or go, to try to be first to the ball?' You will have a split-second to make up your mind. If you decide it's 'Go!', you must 'explode' towards the ball – sprint for it. If you hesitate, chances are you will not get there first.

Be first, be strong – but you have to be quick off the mark, and brave, to steal the ball from the feet of an attacker.

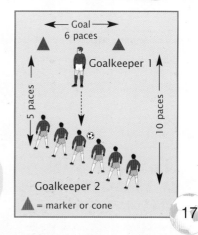

GO FOR IT!

Attack the ball and spread yourself down across the ball. Use a sliding movement.

PRACTICE NO. 1

This drill needs two players. Mark a goal six paces wide and place a ball five paces away.

- You guard the goal. Your pal, goalkeeper 2, stands still just behind the ball.

- When he gives a signal, you rush out to attack the ball. The signal must not be a spoken command.

- The ball is on the ground, so you will have to slide in.

- Next, place the ball slightly further away and repeat. Get the feeling of 'exploding' towards the ball – like a sprinter at the start of a race.

- Have five goes, each time moving further away and from a different angle.

- Now change over and let your pal try. Don't forget, the ball is not moving – you are.

Safety first: Gather the ball to your chest and cover it up to stop it running loose.

BE THE BEST

Gather the ball into your body quickly, then stand up. Be ready to throw or kick the ball out.

Use this diagram to help you practise coming off your line.

← Goal →
6 paces

▲   ▲

Goalkeeper 1

5 paces

10 paces

Goalkeeper 2

▲ = marker or cone

BE THE BEST

If you decide *not* to race out for the ball, make some movements to put off the attacker – sway your hips or move your arms. This will keep him guessing about which way you might move.

PRACTICE NO. 2

I call this one 'Quick on the draw'. There's a Wild West feel to it!

- Using the same size goal as before, the attacker and goalkeeper stand still, five paces from either side of the ball. Wait for a few seconds.

- The goalkeeper decides to stay back or go for the ball. The attacker tries to score.

- Have five goes each, with the ball at a different angle but at the same distance from goal.

- Swap roles. Each of you try being goalkeeper five times.

If there are three of you, the third player sits out and gives the 'start' command. But he can take his turn.

- Watch the action closely, even when you are not in goal. You can always learn from others' mistakes or good points. Watching someone else in goal can give you an idea of how you look in that role.

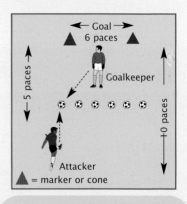

Here's how to set up your practice for 'quick on the draw'.

CLEARANCES

Sometimes a goalkeeper may not have time to catch the ball cleanly, or the ball might be out of reach. At a corner-kick, he might have a crowd of players stopping him getting to the cross. In this case, he may have to punch it clear or deflect it away, to prevent it from being an immediate danger to his goal.

Reach for the stars: Keepers have to be strong and decisive to get there ahead of the crowd.

Use the energy of the ball by punching it back in the direction it came from.

GO FOR IT!

The aim is to get the ball as high, wide and as far away from the goal as possible.

The most important thing it is to get the ball away to safety, as far as possible from your goal. Punching clear is important. If you do not get it away by some distance, it might fall in the path of an attacker and you will not be back in position when he shoots. Sometimes, all you can do is to palm or fingertip the ball over your own crossbar or round a post for a corner. This is not ideal – but it is certainly better than conceding a goal!

PRACTICE NO. 1

Set up a goal six paces wide and mark out two more points as in the diagram.

• The attacker tosses the ball in the air, towards the goalkeeper, from each of the two positions.

• The attacker has five serves from each position.

• When you have mastered this, serve from the other wing.

Toss the ball towards the keeper for him to punch away.

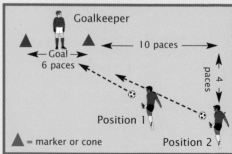

Goalkeeper

← 10 paces →

← Goal →
6 paces

4 paces

Position 1

Position 2

▲ = marker or cone

Keep fists together to make the best contact with the ball.

PRACTICE NO. 2

Now make it more like in a match.

GO FOR IT!

If the ball is catchable, catch it. If it is not, punch it clear. Be decisive.

- Repeat Practice No. 1, but this time get a friend to put the keeper under a bit of pressure.
- We don't want the attacker charging in, but he could make a jump to try to head the high ball.

It is important to get the distance when you punch.

BE THE BEST

The extra player is now a distraction to the goalkeeper. Concentrate hard, and don't be put off by having someone close by going for the same ball.
When you get really confident, the server should move the markers slightly further away and can try to kick the ball.

Safety first: If it is not safe to catch the ball, flip it over the bar.

PRACTICE NO. 3

In a game, you often see a goalkeeper clearing the danger by pushing a cross over his own crossbar. This is because the ball is so close to the goal and, if he doesn't punch the ball properly (it could be wet or muddy), he might end up punching it into his own net!

You will need a junior goal for this one, though the rest of the set-up remains the same. Put markers down either side of the goal.

• Ask the attacker to serve the ball as close to the bar as possible. See if he can make it bounce on the top of the crossbar.

• When you have mastered this, put the goalkeeper under pressure by using a friend to challenge for the serve. Later, try serving the ball by kicking it, as you would in a real match.

The attacker must serve the ball as close to the crossbar as possible.

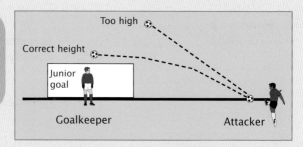

Too high

Correct height

Junior goal

Goalkeeper

Attacker

GO FOR IT!

The goalkeeper should have the palm of the hand facing the bar and behind the ball. Push it over the bar with your palm and fingers – don't punch.

You might concede a corner, but a missed punch or catch could give away a goal.

DID YOU KNOW?

Only two goalkeepers have captained a World Cup winning side. Giampiero Combi led Italy to their first title in 1934. Dino Zoff skippered the Italians to victory in 1982.

FIRST LINE OF **ATTACK**

When the goalkeeper makes a save and gathers the ball, he becomes an instant attacker. His speed of thought and the way he 'passes' the ball can affect the success of his team's next attack. A goalkeeper is ideally placed to see the whole pitch in front of him. If he is clever, he will also know the sort of runs and positions his teammates like to take up when he has the ball in his hands, ready to start a quick attack.

'Quick, throw it!' Where would you pass the ball?

Kick to an attacker

Long throw to mid-fielder

Short throw to defender

Goalkeeper

Ask yourself these questions...

1 Can I put my forwards in with a chance to score? This may mean a long kick behind the other defence.

2 Can I get the ball safely to a forward? A long kick will be needed.

3 Can I get the ball safely to one of my midfield players? This will mean an accurate throw.

4 Can I get the ball safely to a defender? This means a short, accurate throw.

Rolling the ball out: Sometimes your target pass is close – but you still need to take care.

PRACTICE NO. 1

Set up two goals, six paces wide and 15 paces apart.

- Try scoring against your partner by throwing the ball into his or her goal. Have ten throws each, for round 1.

- Have two more rounds, changing ends after each round. The winner is the one who lets in the fewest number of goals!

GO FOR IT!

Make the save, compose yourself, then throw...

BE THE BEST

Try out the following throwing actions:

- Overarm, like bowling

- Under-arm, like ten-pin bowling.

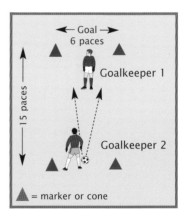

← Goal →
6 paces

Goalkeeper 1

15 paces

Goalkeeper 2

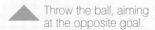 = marker or cone

Throw the ball, aiming at the opposite goal.

GO FOR IT!

Lean into your throw – this will give you more power and accuracy.

PRACTICE NO. 2

When throwing the ball to your teammates, make it easy for them to control it. The ball should not go too high.

This practice will encourage a flat delivery of the ball. Remember – the longer your teammate has to wait for the ball, the less time he will have to control it before being tackled.

Make a goal, four paces wide. Mark out two squares either side of it, each two paces wide. Do the same, 15 paces away, as in the diagram.

- Stand in the centre of your goal and throw the ball so it bounces in either of the opposing goalkeeper's squares. You score a point each time you are successful.

- The goalkeeper will be trying to prevent the ball going in either of his marked boxes.

- Have ten goes each. Who will be the champion?

BE THE BEST

Keep the flight of your throw low – but try to get it into the other box without it bouncing.

Aim for the squares on either side of the goalkeeper.

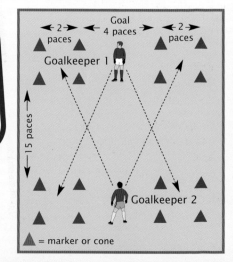

26

Watch closely: Drop kicking the ball means timing your kick just as the ball touches the ground.

GO FOR IT!

Clench your toes the instant you make contact with the ball, for power.

PRACTICE NO. 3

Set up two goals, 25 paces apart. Take turns to try to score. Have five shots using one of the methods below, then five more using the other methods.

- **Volley:** The ball is kicked before it touches the ground after being served from your hands.

- **Drop-volley or half-volley:** You make contact with the ball just as it is it touches the floor having been served from your hands.

- **Ground strike:** The ball is still or rolling on the pitch.

BE THE BEST

- Keep your eye on the ball at all times.
- Make contact with the centre of the ball.
- Strike the ball with your instep (laces).
- Keep your ankle firm.

27

Eyes up: Concentrate on finding the best option quickly.

PRACTICE NO. 4

Set up a goal, six paces wide. Mark four small boxes around a goalkeeper, 25 paces from your own goal. The second keeper stands anywhere he likes inside the blue zone marked on the diagram.

- Goalkeeper 2 tries to score against his pal. When goalkeeper 1 saves, he must try to 'score' by throwing the ball in one of the four 'box goals'. The other goalkeeper should try to stop him.

- Have five goes each and then change. Repeat twice.

- The winner is the one who scores the most 'box goals'.

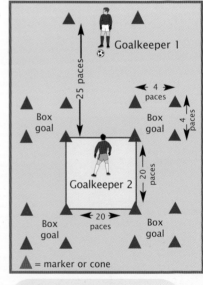

25 paces

Goalkeeper 1

4 paces

4 paces

Box goal

Box goal

20 paces

Goalkeeper 2

20 paces

Box goal

Box goal

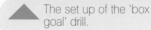
= marker or cone

The set up of the 'box goal' drill.

THE SKILLS **TEST**

Test all of your new skills in a competition with your mates. The champion is the one who wins most of the nine rounds! In each round you will need to call on many of the key points you have learned.

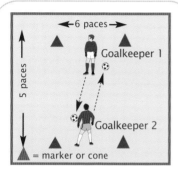

ROUND 1

Measure out the pitch and goals.

- Take shots at each other.
- The first to make three saves is the winner.

One on one: Go through the drills with a friend.

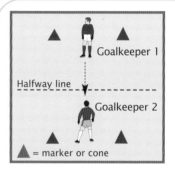

ROUND 2

Use the same pitch as round 1.

- Goalkeeper 1 tries to dribble against the opposing keeper, who can only touch the ball once it crosses the halfway line.
- Have four attacks each – the one who makes the most saves, wins.

ROUND 3

As soon as the attacker moves, the keeper can rush forward.

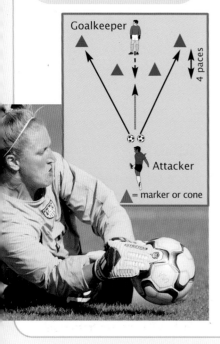

You need one goal and a smaller goal marked out in front.

- The goalkeeper stands on the goal-line.

- The attacker has two footballs. He must try to shoot through the small goal. With the second ball, he goes for the bigger goal.

- The moment the attacker starts to move, the ball is 'live' and the goalkeeper can rush forward to try to save in the smaller goal.

- He will need to get up quickly to defend his bigger goal from the second shot.

- Have three goes at each goal – big and small – before changing sides. The person with the most saves wins.

ROUND 4

Play this non-stop for three minutes.

- Each goalkeeper is allowed only two touches of the ball to score.

- As soon as one goalkeeper touches the ball, the other can narrow the angle. If a save is made and the ball rebounds into play, the game goes on.

- If a player touches the ball more than twice, a penalty is awarded. The kick is taken 10 paces from goal.

- The winner is the one who lets in the fewest goals.

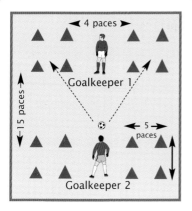

ROUND 5

Set up four squares, each five paces square, as marked.

- One goalkeeper stands in the space between the squares and tries to throw the ball so it bounces in either of the opposite squares. They are defended by the other goalkeeper.

- Have four throws each to score in the goal zones.

- The ball must bounce in the zone to count.

ROUND 7

Mark an area as shown and place two balls as marked.

- The attacker rolls the ball forward and shoots.

- The goalkeeper tries to save. But if the ball rolls outside the zone, or goes wide, both players go for the second ball, which is five paces from goal.

- If the shot with this second ball rebounds off the keeper, the attacker has four seconds to score or the ball is ruled dead.

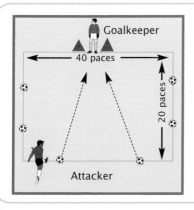

ROUND 6

Set up a goal, six paces wide. Mark an area 40 paces by 20 paces, as shown.

- The attacker will have six shots from different positions around the zone.

- After six, change roles.

- The winner is the goalkeeper making the most saves.

ROUND 8

Two keepers stand side by side and an attacker is ten paces away.

- As the attacker releases the ball, the two goalkeepers try to clear the ball or grab it.
- The goalkeepers have three more goes, starting from different stances – kneeling, sitting down and, finally, laying on their stomach.
- The most saves or clearances wins.

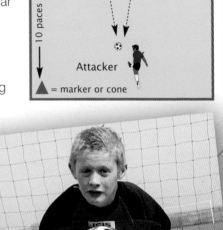

2 Goalkeepers

← 6 paces →

10 paces

Attacker

▲ = marker or cone

Simply the best: The goalkeeper with the most saves wins the competition.

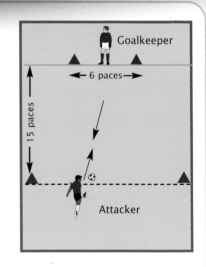

ROUND 9

The attacker starts 15 paces from goal with the ball.

- As soon as he dribbles the ball forward, the goalkeeper can come off his line.
- The attacker has five seconds to score.
- If the attack breaks down – a missed shot or a save – a new attack starts from outside the 15-pace line.
- Swap roles after five tries. The most saves wins.

Goalkeeper

← 6 paces →

15 paces

Attacker